Passing the 11+ with NLP

NLP strategies for supporting your 11 plus student

Judy Bartkowiak

Carolyn Fitzpatrick

Paperback ISBN 978-1-907685-73-6

ePub ISBN 978-1-907685-74-3

Mobipocket/Kindle ISBN 978-1-907685-75-0

Published in the UK by MX Publishing

335 Princess Park Manor, Royal Drive, London, N11 3GX

www.mxpublishing.co.uk

Cover design by www.staunch.com

ABOUT THE AUTHORS

Judy Bartkowiak is an NLP Kids Specialist and runs a life coaching practice in South Buckinghamshire where she lives with her four children. She is the author of 'Teach Yourself: Be a happier parent with NLP' (Hodder Education).

Judy ran a Nursery School for 7 years when her children were pre-school and believes passionately in teaching NLP to children so that they have the skills to achieve all they want in life.

Carolyn Fitzpatrick is an 11+ tutor based in Buckinghamshire, tutoring 27 children a week. She taught English and Drama at Primary and Secondary school level before becoming an 11+ tutor ten years ago. She too ran a Nursery School for 15 years while her children were growing up. She says,

"I love seeing the development of the children not just educationally but socially and emotionally as well. Some children come here who won't say two words to me and have no self confidence. I see them growing over the year and believing that they can actually attempt the questions. Then I have the other extreme where I have some over-confident children who talk so much that they don't take in any information and I see them settle down and begin to get into a real work ethic of chatting to me at the beginning and the end of the lesson but during it they sit and listen and do what they need to do."

CONTENTS

Page

INTRODUCTION

NLP is a completely different way of viewing your world. Once you have been introduced to the NLP way of thinking and communicating it will seem like you've come home. It is respectful of others and more importantly of yourself and your 11+ student because it is positive.

John Grinder and Richard Bandler developed what they came to call NLP from a combination of Virginia Satir's Family Therapy, Franz Perls' Gestalt Therapy and the work of Milton Erickson in the area of language patterns. What Grinder and Bandler added was the idea of coding excellence by observing how effective people communicated and forming ground rules that would bring these results to anyone who applied them. These ground rules are what we call NLP or Neuro Linguistic Programming.

We have used these to underpin the 11+ strategies you want to know about in order to support your child throughout the preparation for the 11+ exam.

This workbook is designed first and foremost to be a practical workbook for you to use to support your 11+ student on a day to day basis.

It is specifically geared towards mums and dads as we feel it is they who will be supporting the 11+ students on a daily basis although it will also make interesting reading for grandparents, teachers and carers who have regular contact with children sitting the 11+ and who want to help them.

We have referred to your child as 'him' throughout the book in order to tie in with the boy on the cover and for consistency .... and perhaps because we know from experience that boys of this age seem to find it harder to focus on work because they'd much rather be outside kicking a ball around!

Obviously all the contents of this book relate to girls as well so just substitute 'she' or 'her' for 'he' and 'him' when you are reading it with your daughter.

One of the questions asked by mums on a regular basis is how much they should be involved in their children's 11+ preparation. We recommend taking a middle road.

Some mums are just not interested; they sign their child up for 11+ tuition and take no further interest in the lessons or homework at all. Other parents are on the case for the whole year. Then there is the middle road where the parents make sure homework is done, vocabulary learnt, reading done, and that, we feel, is the ideal level of involvement. Children need to know that their parent is interested in what they're doing and that they are both working towards the same goal which is to get them to the school where they want to be.

I had a little boy one year who was never going to pass from the moment he walked in the door. He actually didn't seem to care whether he passed or not. But he could have done so much better for himself. He could have felt so much better about himself and his confidence. If he did homework it was all wrong and nobody ever looked at it, nobody helped him. He was one of the only children I've had who didn't progress.

Little and often seems to work best rather than expecting them to sit down for an hour and a half, they literally need ten minute bursts.

At the start of Year 5, work earnestly on times tables and reading, nothing else up to Christmas. It doesn't matter if they are reading a comic, a newspaper or a Dr Who annual, so long as it is words on paper. Get them to read and extend their vocabulary.

Give them a reason to do things, so rather than sitting down and saying 'we're doing this workbook' make it relevant to their daily life.

For example, if they want to buy 7 toys at 50p how much change would they get for a £10 note? Encourage them to understand why tables are so useful. We do not recommend looking at 11+ papers at home until May.

If you know what compound words, homophones and similes are, this all helps your 11+ child because you can notice them in sentences and point them out to your child as examples. These will be covered in the literacy chapter.

Teach your child to visualise the letters in words because this is a very important skill for the 11+. NLP has a great spelling strategy that is covered in the first chapter on how children learn.

Encourage them to have a go at every question when they do practice papers because it doesn't matter if they get a question wrong. What they will learn from this and the feedback they get will be how to get it right. There is no learning from no response.

Another way you can help them is by practising at home a good way of sitting at a desk that will enable them to work effectively. We see children sitting sideways or crouched up or with their head on their hand. The 11+ paper lasts 50 minutes so learning how to sit comfortably and resourcefully at a desk is a handy skill to have. We suggest that the hand not used for writing needs to be used to point at the question to focus them in so they don't lose their place. Once shown, children are really surprised how it helps them.

This book will show you how your child learns best, how to build their confidence, set goals and how to tackle the different types of question in the 11+.

CHAPTER 1: THE GROUND RULES

Neuro Linguistic Programming has a number of presuppositions or ground rules that personally, we have found life changing. We hope you do too.

Read through them before you start reading the book because they underpin all the tools and techniques covered in the different chapters.

We have written the ground rules specifically for you to apply to your own life and know that you will pass them on to your child by example which is how they learn best.

1) *If you always do what you've always done then you will always get what you've always got*

This is by far the most important in our opinion because it states quite clearly that you can't change other people's behaviour so if you want a different result you must change your own.

By changing what you do, you can affect a different result. So if you feel your child is not working hard enough, spending long enough on his home work or getting good marks at school then by changing what you do, you will influence this result.

Maybe you've had the experience of constantly saying the same thing to your child. We've all done it! I suppose we hope against hope that one day the 'penny will drop' and they'll do what we ask. Well it won't and they don't. We need to change if we want to get a different and better result because what we have been doing is not working.

Equally of course if your child keeps getting results he is not pleased with then he needs to change what he does and how he does it.

Because we do what we do and say what we say because of our beliefs; if we want to change what we do and say we have to also change those beliefs. We're not talking here about your values and identity, we're just talking about the premises you have about what you do. We will be looking at this in more detail in the book.

Some beliefs limit your choices of behaviour so by revisiting them you increase your options. This enables you to change your behaviour and get the result you want.

2) *You have the resources to do whatever you want to do*

Both you and your child already have a huge resource of skills that you have built up since birth and each one enables you to apply it in different ways by transferring it to the application you need it for.

Believing he has the resources he needs is an empowering belief to take on board because it encourages him to look within himself to find his skills, knowing that he does have them somewhere.

We will explore skills and beliefs later in the book. For now, it is enough to believe you have the resources. If you find that difficult at the moment, act 'as if' you believe it. Acting 'as if' is a way of 'trying it on for size' as it were.

3) *If someone else can do it, you can too*

Nothing is impossible, your child can acquire new skills and hone existing ones by modelling (or copying) them in someone who demonstrates that skill with excellence.

Have you ever regarded someone and thought 'I wish I could do that'? We take on the belief that we have the resources we need and one of those resources is to copy the qualities and skills we observe in others so that we can replicate it in our own life.

This can be a simple skill like putting on lipstick without a mirror or a more complex one such as knowing your tables. Each skill is broken down into its different parts and we learn and accept the underlying belief that we can do it.

This is a core and unique aspect of NLP which differentiates it from other therapies. There is a whole chapter about it in this book.

16

4) There is no failure only feedback

Every experience he has will have a learning potential for him, including negative experiences. This is just as true for you as well.

Instead of feeling he has failed when things do not go well or if he is dissatisfied with what is going on in his life; encourage him to reframe this by looking at it in a different, positive way to find the positive intention which is for him to learn from it.

Feedback is a resource to help us learn what is working and what could be even better.

How he uses this feedback is his choice. No-one can <u>make</u> him feel an emotion, encourage him to make his own choices about how he chooses to feel and respond.

5) *If you spot it you've got it*

When we notice a quality (or a failing) in someone else, this is because in some way we have it too which is how we can recognise it.

When your child observes a quality he admires in someone else, ask him, 'and how are <u>you</u> like that as well?' It may be in another aspect of his life. Be curious with him and explore everything he does so together you can find that skill.

It may be that you have noticed it and need to point out what you have observed that shows him how he has that quality.

Later in the book we'll talk about how we can transfer the quality or skill to where we need it now.

6) If you try, you won't succeed

How often do we say 'Just <u>try</u> that question' or 'Can you <u>try</u> to concentrate?' Are we acknowledging that they won't succeed? Do we really mean that we want them to <u>try</u> or do we just want them to get on and 'do it?'

Reword your request without the word 'try' and note the different response.

There is built-in failure in the word 'try'.

Just 'do it'.

7) The map is not the territory

How you see the world is different from how your child sees it. This is because of the millions of little bits of input we receive into our unconscious mind; we each select what we bring to our conscious mind.

We each select differently according to our experiences, values and beliefs and our internal referencing system (VAK). We will learn more about that in the first chapter.

What we select becomes our map but it is only <u>our</u> map of the territory and we need to be aware that other people's maps are different and yet just as valid. Your child's map is certainly different to yours so you will have greater rapport and affect your result when you connect with his map by stepping into his shoes and seeing his life as he sees it.

Be curious.

8) Look for the positive intention

We do things for a reason. We have a positive intention behind our behaviour as does our child.

If we think about what is going on in our life that we don't like, think about what we get from this. There will be some sort of pay off.

Question what other behaviours could give you the same positive intention with more satisfactory results for you.

Similarly, if we see behaviour in our child that we don't want, consider other ways for them to get the pay off without giving the behaviour. The starting point for this is finding out what their positive intention is.

9) Mind the gap

We often react spontaneously from an associated state. This means that we take what our children say and do very personally.

11+ year can be an emotional roller coaster. Our children will probably get stressed at some point and so will we. They will say hurtful things they don't really mean. So how do we 'mind the gap?'

Before responding, stop and consider how an impartial bystander might see or hear the situation differently. We can do this by imagining we are a fly on the wall looking at the situation and hearing what has been said from a 'disassociated' position.

It gives us the chance to experience the stimulus objectively and then we have a choice about how we want to respond rather than react spontaneously.

10) The person with the most flexibility controls the system

Flexibility in this context is based on understanding how we think and the patterns of behaviour that we use because of the way we process the inputs that enter our unconscious and conscious mind.

What you will learn in this book and pass on to your child will enable you to have the sort of rapport with him that will give you the flexibility to choose your options in order to get the results you want.

Neuro Linguistic Programming teaches us that we have options in how we respond to what is being said to us, how others behave with us, our own self talk and behaviour. These choices give us flexibility.

The more flexibility we have, the more we are in rapport. This rapport enables us to get what we want according to our desired outcome.

By having a desired outcome in every situation we focus on what we want rather than being passive and simply getting what's given. This way we can influence the outcome using rapport and the flexibility we have from knowing how we and others are processing.

Neuro Linguistic Programming is how our minds process external inputs, how these affect what we say and do and what become patterns of behaviour that either work for us or not.

The challenge of this book is to learn how we can use this knowledge to get the results we want and show our children how to do it too so they can get the results they want.

NLP also encourages us to be 'ecological' this means that we need to always bear in mind how what we do affects others because the changes we want may have adverse effects on those around us.

CHAPTER 2. LEARNING STYLES

At any point in time our unconscious mind receives about 2 million inputs but our conscious mind can only process between 7 and 9. This is why when we go to visit a Grammar School with our 11+ student each of us will notice different things and filter out other aspects of the school.

I recently took my Year 5 son to visit a Grammar school and it was as if we'd been to completely different schools! He noticed the food in the canteen (pizza!), the dramatic science experiments (they were setting fire to methane bubbles) and the sports facilities.

He must have zoned out during the Headmaster's talk because he didn't remember anything about it!

How we filter these inputs depends on our experiences of the world, our values and beliefs and our internal representation.

It is our internal representation I want to focus on in this chapter. There are 3 basic ones: Visual, Auditory and Kinaesthetic. We can use all three although our child will favour one of them and this will be how they learn best.

By knowing which they use most, you know how best to support them, how to use language that will motivate them and how to work with them on 11+ papers in a way that they will be able to understand immediately because your words will connect with the way they process information.

How do you know which your child is?

Your child is visual if he is arty, notices what he sees and is more aware than others of how he and other people look. He will be visual if he uses imagery in his language and remembers what he has seen rather than what is said to him.

A visual child will say things like 'Look at this!', 'Have you seen this?', and 'I see what you mean'. They will be observant and notice differences and patterns so the non verbal reasoning tests may be easier for him than for an auditory or kinaesthetic child especially if he focuses on what he sees on the page.

He may well be a good reader and be able to imagine what he reads. He will notice new words and visualise what they mean in the context of the sentence.

He will break words up visually and notice prefixes such as 'inter' and 'un', 'in' and so on. He will also notice compound words and be able to see the two parts and imagine what the combination of the two would mean eg motorcycle. Words that look the same but sound different such as refuse and refuse might be more confusing and take more practise.

He will also work best on homework and practice papers in an area he finds visually attractive.

Your visual child will also have a memory of his chosen Grammar School that is visual and based on what he saw rather than what the Headmaster said in his talk. Focus on his visual memories to motivate him and encourage him to visualise himself being there.

I was asked to see an 11+ student, Max, who was feeling stressed about the forthcoming exam and met him at home with his mum. We talked about when he felt most uneasy and I could tell he was visual by his language patterns.

He told me that his mum insisted that he worked at the kitchen table in 'exam conditions' because she was kinaesthetic. Max however did not like the look of the table where he worked because it had scratches and marks on it. From where he sat he could glimpse out of the corner of his eye, the television flickering through the dividing door and this distracted him. He was also distracted by other people walking into the kitchen.

I asked him where he'd prefer to work and he showed me the playroom which was very tidy and he said he felt more relaxed there and would work better because he wouldn't be visually distracted. He sat down and showed me that what he could see if he looked up from the sofa was attractive.

29

His mother was reluctant because she felt this wasn't exam conditions working from the sofa but was prepared to give it a go.

I spoke to them a few weeks later and she reported that he was much calmer and well prepared for the exam.

By now you will have worked out if your child is visual and also whether you are visual. Be aware of your own internal preference because this will influence your own choice of words and what is important to you. If your child is not visual, his needs will be different. Awareness gives you flexibility to choose the type of language and conditions for work that will connect best with your child.

An auditory child will notice what he hears and will probably be quite musical. He will be chattier than the visual child and speak slower and with more thought about the words he uses.

Because of the focus on words, your auditory child will have picked up on words people use around him and his vocabulary will be based on those words. You can encourage this by using words that he will have in the 11+ paper and telling him what they mean. He will remember these more easily if you say them rather than by his reading them on the page.

Auditory children learn well with music in the background and often talk to themselves.

It is extremely important for children to know their times tables thoroughly for the 11+ so for an auditory child a times tables CD played in the car with songs will be easier to learn than seeing them written down.

Auditory children enjoy stories being read to them so to increase their vocabulary, read to them at bedtime, stories from books with more advanced vocabulary and sentence construction than they would normally read to themselves.

Point out and explain new words and notice types of words like nouns, adjectives and verbs that are unfamiliar as well as words that look the same but mean different things such as 'refuse' (rubbish and say no) emphasising the different pronunciation (emphasis on the first part of the word for 'rubbish' and the second part of the word for 'say no'.

I teach auditory children best by making funny sounds out of words for example where there are words with oo we make 'ooo' sounds and pretend to be ghosts. So every time we saw a double o we went oooo.

This really helps children who are struggling with reading. They'd expect me to give them a page and say 'read that' and they are thinking 'I can't' instead we look at the pictures and say what's happening in this story and pick out some words like 'lolly' and think about other similar words like 'golly' 'holly' 'molly' and maybe jump up and down while we did it. So every time they saw the word 'lolly' they remember when they were jumping up and down and being really funny.

Your auditory child will focus on what he heard at the open day for the Grammar School of his choice. He will remember the talks, what was said, any musical event there and what he heard other people say about the school.

When you want to motivate him, remind him of auditory memories.

If your child is auditory and you are not, it may not be the most natural thing for you to sound out words and focus on sounds so when you are working on practice papers together, be prepared to read out instructions and talk through examples.

Kinaesthetic children are active and fidgety and would rather be doing anything than studying so make work times short and keep up whatever sport or activities they do.

Lois is a fidget. She can't sit still on her chair and often ends up kneeling and leaning right over the table. She tends to invade the others' workspace. She also talks continually - very interesting stories but nothing to do with the 11+ and very distracting for the others. Her listening skills are poor and her concentration span is short.

Firstly I will allot a few minutes as they arrive for her to tell me what she has been doing during the week. She is then asked to save another story until the end of the lesson when I will listen again. If she starts to story tell during the lesson I stop her immediately. If she talks at the same time as me I continue and then she finds that she cannot recall what I have said.

She begins to realise the benefits of listening and talking as separate entities. I encourage her to sit down with her feet under the table and each time she kneels I remind her and she sits back down. This begins to occur less and less.

I use a great deal of visualisation while I am talking so she has to look as well as listen and this focuses her concentration more fully. After 6 weeks she is used to the routine and finds that her work improves as she is able to sit still.

She has improved her sitting, listening and looking skills and is surprised how much easier she finds the work.

I ask mum to follow a similar routine while she is doing her homework or even when they are sitting at the dinner table as a family.

Your kinaesthetic child will be more aware of temperature than other children and will be distracted if he is too hot or too cold so provide a warm place to work in the winter and a cool one in the summer.

These children learn best by doing, so practise and practise again. They respond well to working on a computer because it is interactive so use whatever 11+ material you can find online.

They also work well in pairs, testing each other and working through examples together so group tutoring works especially well for them as well as getting them to buddy up with another child with whom they can work on practice papers.

Your kinaesthetic child will use phrase like 'I get this' or 'I'll have a stab at that question'. Their words are action orientated and relate to doing things like 'Hold on', 'I need to grab a pen' and so on.

They remember feelings and experiences so they will remember what happened at the open day at the Grammar School and what they felt.

My kinaesthetic daughter visited several Grammar Schools and didn't like any of them because they didn't 'feel' right. One was too claustrophic (it was a very old building), one felt too big and sprawled out, another felt dirty. I despaired. Then we visited St Bernard's and from the moment we stepped in through the entrance she was smitten. She squeezed my hand and said 'Mummy I really want to come here, it feels right'. She was completely motivated to go there and was happy throughout her Secondary Education. I never heard her complain once about the school.

You will need to ensure that your kinaesthetic child builds their visual and auditory skills in preparation for the 11+ because they won't be natural readers, preferring instead to be out doing things, mostly sport.

If you are not kinaesthetic but your child is, be prepared to spend more time working together than perhaps you needed for a previous non kinaesthetic sibling.

Meta Programmes

So we have learnt the three internal representations and know what this means in terms of our children's learning styles and how best to communicate with them.

However, there is another facet to this. According to NLP there are also Meta Programmes that we run. This is more about personality. There are a number of variables so I'll just focus on those I believe are most relevant to the 11+ and learning.

It is a fascinating subject and if you'd like to read more about it then may I direct you to Sue Knight's book NLP at work or my own Teach Yourself: Be a happier parent with NLP both of which include a larger selection of Meta Programmes which are more relevant to adults.

Here are the ones I think will be helpful to you

<u>Big chunk/small chunk</u>

No this isn't about chocolate!

If your child is 'big chunk' he will think broad brush in concepts rather than detail. If he draws he will tend to just draw an outline and his eyes will glaze over if you go into detail about what the plans are for the weekend or your holiday.

He just wants basic essential information and he will work out the rest himself. He won't read instructions or the rules of a game, may just guess how to put the Lego model together and only vaguely measure ingredients if you're cooking together.

This child will find going through the 11+ paper quite tedious if you spend a long time explaining the detail of how to tackle the question.

Instead take one type of question, explain it briefly and then let him do the set.

If your child enjoys detail he will be 'small chunk'. He will be interested in the detailed instructions for how to do each question type and probably ask you to explain it again and again until he has fully understood.

He will probably take the practice paper much slower than the big chunk child, being careful and methodical, wanting to be sure he has considered the question fully.

Speed may be a problem for him rather than accuracy so the approach may be to encourage him to answer all the questions he can do easily first and circle the numbers of those he wants to return to at the end.

Choices/Process

A 'choices' child is one who likes options.

Multiple choice suits them just fine except they sometimes find it hard to make a decision so for them they may be better advised to tackle the question first, decide on the answer and then select it from the choices.

This child likes to choose and enjoys the process of choosing so he may be undecided for some time about which school he likes. He will weigh up all the options, the pros and cons and want to see more schools than the 'procedures' child who just wants to get the job done.

The procedures child will be a list maker with lots to do and no time for choices about them. He will work his way steadily through the paper and answer every question rather than spend time deciding which question to do next. There won't be any danger of him missing one out because this is a process for him.

Towards/Away from

'Towards' children have things they want to do, they have plans and ideas, goals to meet and tend to be achievement orientated. They will set their mind to getting what they want and won't think about the consequences of failure.

By contrast, the 'away from' child fears failure and expends energy in avoiding things. They will want to avoid failing the 11+, fear types of questions coming up that they feel less comfortable with and steer a relatively careful path through life avoiding risk.

This child will be best prepared for the 11+ by ensuring all worries are sorted by preparation so they won't have any unpleasant surprises in the test.

Internally/externally referenced

An internally referenced child does things because they want to do them and because they meet their goals and values. They won't be swayed by others and so long as they themselves want to pass the 11+ they will do the work that's required.

An externally focused child will be influenced by others and rarely check in with what they want for themselves. If it is you rather than they who wants this goal then their commitment will be to pleasing you which is fine but just be aware that this is their motivation.

Ask them 'what do you want?' and go through the goal setting exercise because internal referencing of goals tends to result in a higher pass mark because they are doing it because they want to do it.

Match/Mismatch

Some children notice what they have in common with others and some notice what is different. You can instantly tell a mismatch child because they tend to contradict you!

Much of the 11+ paper, verbal and nonverbal reasoning, is concerned with finding what's similar and what is different. Once you know your child's preference you will know exactly how to help him with this.

Associated/Disassociated

An 'associated' child will be more emotional and sensitive, take things to heart and be anxious to please. He will get disheartened if he can't do something and take it quite personally.

A 'disassociated' child will be slightly more distant and be able to get things into perspective without getting upset by pitfalls. This child will cope with the pressure of the exam situation better than the associated child because they can separate their emotions from the situation.

It's unlikely that your child will be totally one or the other and you will know how well your own child copes with pressure. You can use anchoring to anchor a calm state and this is covered in the section on State Management.

Rapport

Rapport is about getting on with other people and connecting with them. If you and your child are in rapport you will easily be able to support him by matching his VAK and Meta Programmes. If you don't there will be a lot of pencil throwing and door slamming and it isn't going to work. It's going to be 'I'm not doing this, I'm going upstairs, it's goodbye...gone'.

The best way to get this rapport is to match the preference of the person you are talking to.

1) Body language; how they are standing or sitting, the angle of their head, the amount of eye contact they are giving you and how they move.
2) How they speak, the length of their sentences, tone of voice, pitch, volume and pace.
3) The words they use; are they visual, auditory or kinaesthetic. Reflect the same words back to them. If they speak a different language this will also help with comprehension.

If you need to be in rapport with someone with a different Meta programme, match theirs and you will be speaking the same language.

Sometimes this isn't enough because if you need a choices child to make a decision you need to take the lead. You do this by deciding what procedure you need to happen and offer them limited choices within that such as whether they have a drink of water or milk while they do their work.

Similarly, if you need to present a 'big chunk' idea such as going to Grammar School to your child who is 'small chunk' they will want all the detail in order to buy into it. If he needs detail but you are presenting broad concepts, chunk down by telling him specific detail.

If it is you who is 'small chunk' and want to persuade your child who is 'big chunk' then you will need to 'chunk up' by asking yourself 'what does this mean?' 'Let's look at the bigger picture' or 'how does this relate to........?'

A child who is worried about leaving his friends may quote 'away from' problems, things that he will miss and potential problems or niggles. Ask them what they do want, 'So what we're aiming for is......?'

How do you know if you are in rapport? You'll know it, feel it, see it and hear it because you'll be matching each other and communicating effectively.

CHAPTER 3: BUILDING LEARNING SKILLS

We've gathered some NLP strategies in this section which we hope you will find helpful as more general 11+ preparation. Specific Literacy and Numeracy preparation is towards the end of the book.

1) NLP spelling strategy

According to Olive Hickmott and Andrew Bendefy in their excellent book (also published by MX Publishing) 'Seeing Spells Achieving',

"In our experience, 100% of those who struggle with words don't use their powers of visualisation to see words."

This is the basis of the NLP Spelling Strategy which is explained in full detail with plenty of exercises and case studies in their book.

Visualisation is the process whereby we capture and hold a mental image in our mind and refer to it when we spell. Here's how to do it with your child.

First get them thinking about how they visualise. Ask him to imagine his favourite TV character. Can he picture the character in his head? Ask him to describe what he has in his mind. What does it look like? Tell him that this is called 'visualising'.

Now let's apply it to spelling.

Step 1. Let's start with some very basic 3 letter words that he can confidently spell e.g. cat, dog, cow, pig.

Step 2. Imagine a picture of a cat in your mind and write the letters c-a-t on the cat's body somewhere. It will be easier for a right handed child to look up and to his left to do this (opposite for a left- handed child)

Step 3. Break State – this means switch his attention for a moment on to something else.

Step 4. Now ask him to imagine his cat again. Has it still got c-a-t on its body? Yes? Ask him to read the letters backwards out loud as he is picturing them t-a-c. Then do it forwards and then backwards again. This ensures that the sound of the letters and the visual picture of them on the image are linked in his head.

Step 5. Ask him if he'd like to change anything about the way they are written? Would he like to write them in his favourite colour, make them larger, make them capitals or change where they are written?

Step 6. Do the same with the other 3 letter words. Spelling them backwards is really important because it means he is doing this visually. This may not seem important now with 3 letter words but believe me, it will be when he gets to longer words.

Step 7. Let the image of the animals fade to just leave the writing.

Step 8. Now move on to 4 letter words, 5, 6 and 7 letter words. When you get to eight letter words use compound words with two different parts making up the whole, each a word in its own right so handcuff he would picture the word 'h-a-n-d' and then 'c-u-f-f'.

Pictures work well for nouns where he can picture the image however he will also need to spell adjectives and verbs of course. He may find this approach works better for those.

Step 1. Write the word he wants to spell on a post-it note and put it on the wall in front of him.

Step 2. Ask him to look at the word and spell it out loud.

Step 3. Now ask him to imagine the word in his head.

Step 3. Then with the word covered up ask him to spell it backwards, forwards and backwards again.

Building memory skills

Ask your child to write down a list of 10 nouns (objects) for the sake of an example here's my list based on what is in my office.

Mug

Phone

Pen

Book

Computer

Bagpuss pen holder

Picture

Handbag

Photo frame

Waste paper bin

Next you ask them to make up a story including the objects in the order of the list. Here's my story by way of example:

I picked up my mug while I was on the phone but I couldn't find my pen. I eventually found it inside a book by the computer. It should be in the Bagpuss pen holder. My friend is telling me about her new handbag so I draw a picture of it and then add a photo frame round it. It's so bad I throw it in the waste paper bin.

By relating one object to the next it is easier to remember the list.

There are a number of words that regularly come up in 11+ papers and these will be covered later in the literacy chapter. This memory game is a good way of remembering them.

<u>Pelminism</u>

Lay out a pack of shuffled cards on the table in a square with neat rows.

Each player then takes it in turn to turn over two cards. If they are the same e.g. two sevens, they keep them and have another turn until the two cards are not the same. Then it is the other person's go. You can play with as many people as you want.

The idea is to remember what the cards are and where they are so you can make the pairs by memory of their position rather than by chance.

This helps the kinaesthetic child to build their memory and concentration. They can do it on their own as well and time themselves as to how long it takes to get the pack off the table and into matching pairs.

<u>Kim's Game</u>

Put out 10 objects on a tray and show your child the tray for one minute. Then cover it up and ask them to write down every object they remember seeing on the tray. You can make this more difficult by asking them to also write down the colour, size and order left to right of the objects.

Being aware of order and position will help them with 11+ skills and it will also build concentration and speed of processing information.

<u>My Aunty Flo</u>

One person starts by saying 'my Aunty Flo went to market and she bought a....' The next person continues by repeating what the first person said and adding an item. Then each person repeats the list so far and adds an item. The winner is the last person who remembered the list correctly.

There are loads of games on the Internet and ITunes, both numeracy and literacy games and they have levels so that children get a sense of achievement as they move to more advanced levels.

Once you know whether your child is visual, auditory or kinaesthetic you will know how to motivate them and which areas of the 11+ paper they need most help with.

CHAPTER 4: GOAL SETTING

Your child wants to go to a Grammar School, you want them to be happy and go to the school they have chosen. It would seem on the face of it that your goals are in line. If only it were that simple!?

A lot of my mums take their children to see the schools and the children come back saying 'I'd love to go to that school, it was fantastic they had this and that'. The mums say 'right well to get to this school you are actually going to have to work' so they are giving them a goal which is the school. Some couldn't care less but most of them understand that if they want to get there then they have some input into it. They aren't coming for some boring tuition for an hour, they're coming for a reason. It's to get a goal that they want.

To understand your child's goals and thereby their map of the world (because it will undoubtedly be slightly different from yours) use a Time Line.

Introduce it to them as a game and accept everything they say as being from their map not yours.

1) Ask them to imagine a line along the floor stretching from when they were little to when they are older. It doesn't have to be specific in terms of age.

2) Ask them to stand on the place on that line that represents today. How do they feel, what's going well in their life and what could be even better? Overall, what's working for them?

3) Now ask them to go and stand on the point on the line that represents a time when they are in their next school – secondary school. There is no need to specify the school at all.

4) How do they feel now? What's good, what could be even better and what is working overall. It's best to use the same words at

each point on the line. Notice where they are on the line and how far away it seems (to them) from today's point.

5) Then ask them to take another step along the line to where they will go next. This might be a job or University. How do they feel now? What's good, what could be even better and what is working overall?

6) Keep going and let them map out their goals for the future until they can't go any further.

7) Now ask them to go back and stand at today's point. How do they feel now? Repeat the same questions. What's good, what could be even better and what's good overall?

8) Notice the changes in motivation now they have moved up the time line. Is today's point now in a different place, possibly further up

the line? Do they seem more settled within
their own skin?

9) Ask them what they need to do to make that
next step along the line. They will list what
they need to do to get to the next step and
you will notice that they are more motivated
now they can visualise their future and have
ideas about how to make it happen for
themselves.

The importance of this technique is that we are
encouraging your child to visualise their future. If
they can visualise themselves going to Grammar
School and then to University and having an
interesting and fun job with all that this brings then
they are on the way to achieving it. If they can't
even visualise it then it is unlikely to happen. If your
child can't visualise going to Grammar School read
the chapter on Self Esteem and Limiting Beliefs and
then return to this Time Line exercise afterwards.

The Time Line is used a lot in NLP for goal setting. It can also be used for conquering limiting beliefs and accessing skills so we will encounter it again in the next chapter.

You may have come across SMART goals at work. These are goals that are specific, measurable, achievable, realistic and time focussed. The NLP goal setting strategy is similar and I think more useful for children especially those with exam based goals.

1) First and foremost goals need to be POSITIVE

Ask them what they want and write down what they say, exactly and using their own words.

Check that their goal is worded in the positive. Their goal needs to be a 'towards goal' in other words, what they want to achieve rather than what they want to avoid. Together rewrite it as a positive goal if it isn't already.

It needs to be specific too, so what <u>exactly</u> do they want? Rewrite the goal as a specific goal. If it is about going to a Grammar School, which exact school is it they want to go to?

Connor is worried that he is not able to keep up with the others in the group.

He has basic numeracy skills but the others can solve maths problems quicker than him. We talk about interests out of school and discover that they all like and are good at different things. He tells us that he plays the guitar so I suggest that he plays for us for a few minutes - the others are impressed.

We talk about individual goal setting and how each person is good at different things. His numeracy goals are different to the others in the group but each time he achieves them he receives praise and the others in the group are genuinely pleased for him.

We then re-set the goals to stretch him further and after a term look back to see a vast improvement. I suggest that the parent sits down with him each week and reinforces the numeracy that we have covered to make sure that he has understood it and also so that they can follow his progress carefully to spot any areas where he is still struggling so that we can work further on those particular aspects.

2) How will you recognise when you have achieved it? What EVIDENCE do you need to have that shows that you have achieved your goal?

Ask them to think about what they will look like, sound like and feel like, where they will be and what they will be doing when that goal is achieved.

Visualising it and thinking about it is preparing their mind for the fact of having that goal.

A good exercise here is The Circle of Excellence.

This is a great exercise for your 11+ child because it gives them instant confidence or calmness when they need it.

First tell him that he needs to imagine a circle in front of him on the floor.

Step 1. Ask him how we wants to be when he is sitting his 11+ or when he is doing a practice paper. There is no need to prompt him although you can remind him of anything he has said to you about it such as for example 'I wish I didn't feel so scared' or 'I wish I could stop shaking'. You need to encourage him to think about what he does want though! Encourage him to say what he does want to feel and write the words down on a piece of paper or post it notes.

Step 2. Take the first word and ask him 'When do you feel like this?' It may be in another context or it could be related to school or 11+ work.

Step 3. He is going to anchor this feeling so ask him what action he'd like to make to remind himself of this good feeling. Maybe he wants to squeeze his ear lobe or put his thumb and first finger together.

Step 4. Now ask him to remember having that great feeling, what it looked like, sounded like and felt like. When the feeling is strongest, he's to step into his imaginary circle and use the action he's decided upon. When the feeling subsides, take away the action and step back out of the circle and break state – that means give yourself a little shake and think about something else for a moment.

Step 5. Ask him to repeat this a few times until he has made a strong link between the action and the feeling.

Step 6. Now do the same for the other feelings he wants to have and use the same procedure with the same action and stepping into the circle each time.

Step 7. Tell him that whenever he wants these feelings all he has to do is imagine his circle, step into it and make the action. He can take the circle anywhere he wants.

The ideal time to use it is of course just before he sits his 11+ but he can use it for practice papers as well.

The circle of excellence can be used extensively and when he wants to add feelings he can repeat the process.

If he's done the spelling strategy he can anchor the ability to visualise words.

3) When and where do you want to have this resource? What is the CONTEXT?

Now is the time to think about what skills they already have and which skills they want to acquire in order to meet their goal.

The 11+ is not an end in itself although it might feel like that now! The skills they will build through the process of studying for the 11+ exam will stand them in good stead whatever they do and whichever school they go to.

As an 11+ tutor Carolyn has seen time and again how children coming to her first lesson are lacking in confidence and basic 11+ skills and over a the tutoring weeks she watches their confidence and skills grow. They get higher marks at school, feel more self assured and perform better in all subjects as a result of their increased concentration, listening skills and ability to analyse questions.

4) The goal needs to be SELF ACHIEVABLE. You need to have the ability to achieve the goal yourself.

Their goal cannot be dependent on other people whom they cannot control. Whilst their goal might be to get into a particular school but they cannot control that because each year only a certain percentage will get in according to the number of available places, catchment area and other admission criteria.

5) What will be the ADVANTAGES AND DISADVANTAGES of achieving it?

Whilst the advantages of them achieving their goal might seem obvious, ask them to write a list of what advantages they will gain by achieving this goal.

When they achieve their goal there will be disadvantages because there always are. Ask them to list these as well. Whatever they say, accept their answer because it is real to them in their map of the world. Write them on the next page.

Alongside each one ask them for the positive intention of that disadvantage. What that means is that although the disadvantage exists for them, if they imagine that disadvantage is a person, what benefit does it want to give them? For example, a disadvantage of achieving the goal may be that they won't be with their friends again or that they will have to catch a bus to school. If we were to look at what benefit that apparent disadvantage might have it could be to encourage them to make new friends or to gain independence. Once children understand the positive intention of any perceived disadvantages they cease to be barriers to achieving their goal.

Disadvantages   Positive Intention

6) What is the BENEFIT of this outcome?

By achieving their goal, what benefit will they obtain? What will become available to them that was not available before? What values do they have in life that will be met by achieving their goal? How worthwhile will it be? What negative feeling will they no longer have?

Write down the benefits below. Now alongside each one write down what that benefit would do for you.

Benefit 1

....

What would that do for you?

....

And what would that do for you?

....

And what would that do for you?

....

Benefit 2

....

What would that do for you?

....

And what would that do for you?

....

And what would that do for you?

....

Benefit 3

....

What would that do for you?

....

And what would that do for you?

....

And what would that do for you?

....

Now return to your goal and we will do an anchoring exercise that will enable your child to access this well associated goal for him whenever he needs to refocus and recall what he wants when he gets disheartened or lacks the energy to work.

Anchoring Exercise

Is he visual, auditory or kinaesthetic?

First we need to decide on the anchor he will use. An anchor is an image, sound or action (depending on whether he is visual, auditory or kinaesthetic) that he will use to access the goal.

A visual child may want to picture the smile on his face when he reads that he has passed or the letter saying he has passed. An auditory child might want to hear you saying 'well done you've passed' (if he is externally referenced or 'I've passed wow' (if her is internally referenced). A kinaesthetic child may want to give themselves a hug or do a high five.

Let them choose their own anchor as this will work best.

Now ask them to practise the anchor a few times so they can do it easily when they need to. At this point they might decide that what they've chosen may not be suited to being wherever they might be when they need to use it. If that's the case you could suggest another. Many adults use a more discrete one such as making a circle with their thumb and first finger or squeezing their ear lobe.

Then ask them to associate into their goal. This means to think very hard about achieving their goal, what it will look like (visual), sound like (auditory) and feel like (kinaesthetic). As the sensations of achieving their goal are really strong they use their anchor and as the feelings subside they take away the anchor.

Repeat this several times until it becomes automatic for them to re-experience the joy of achievement whenever they use their anchor.

We use anchors for all sorts of feelings, especially to access our skills and resources for self esteem so we will revisit anchoring in the next chapter.

CHAPTER 5: SELF ESTEEM

What stands in the way of your child's success? Possibly the biggest barrier to passing the 11+ is lack of confidence and self belief. The underlying cause of this lack of confidence is limiting beliefs.

Limiting beliefs are all those things your child believes he cannot do.

Let me reassure you though that your child does have all the resources he needs already and just needs to apply them to passing the 11+.

Sometimes they don't realise they have a skill because they have pigeon-holed it into another area of their life.

My son Paul is fiercely competitive on the sports field and wins races, scores goals and tries and runs. He is one of the sportiest boys in his year. Yet when it comes to classwork he is not competitive at all and doesn't seem that bothered about it. He has the competitive resource but it needs to be transferred to where he needs it.

Sit with your child and together write down their skills. Let them start the process and then when they can't think of any more, tell them the skills you have observed in them with the detail of what exactly you have observed so they too can recognise it.

What I can do well　　　*How that will help me pass*

Now for each one, go back through and discuss between you how that skill will help him pass the 11+.

When you've done that, discuss what else he thinks he needs in the way of skills in order to pass it. Write these down here.

What else I need

Are these things that he says he 'can't do'? Challenge these by asking 'what if you could do that?'

Whatever his limiting belief, challenge it by finding examples of where you have noticed that he has done that thing so he can replicate the structure and belief where and when he needs it.

Her mum tells me that Izzy is in the bottom set at school for both literacy and numeracy, that she has low self confidence and a poor memory and will find it difficult to complete any learning homework.

She is very quiet in the lessons and struggling to keep up with the others immediately. The first week mum is proved right and Izzy comes back not having learnt her vocabulary. I look at her notebook where she writes her vocab each week and see that it is extremely neat and well set out. I ask if she minds if I show the other children her book as I would like them to make theirs neater and easier to read, the same as hers.

This is the first time that she is in a position where she has done something 'better' than the others. I suggest to her that as her book is so neat she will be able to learn the words really easily and perhaps she could learn 3 instead of 5.

The next week she comes back having learnt all 5 and feeling very proud of herself. I suggest to mum that she takes a more positive attitude towards her child's learning by finding something to praise her on, and also breaking the work down into small amounts if it is too much for her - just learn half the words really well.

Here's a great technique you can use with him to tackle remaining limiting beliefs. It's called perceptual positioning in NLP. It gives him the opportunity to separate his belief and look at it objectively.

Position 1 is your child. Position 2 is the limiting belief and Position 3 is the impartial observer. Establish three positions or places in a triangle like this.

Position 3

(impartial observer)

X

X   X

Position 1   Position 2

(your child)   (his limiting belief)

Ask him to stand at position 1 and say what gets in the way of what he wants to do.

Tell him to give himself a little shake to break his state or change mood. This is called 'breaking state'.

Now ask him to go to position 2 and imagine he is that limiting belief and he's to tell position 1 what he knows and what he has observed that shows that he <u>can</u> do this thing.

Ask him to break state again and go to position 3 to comment on what he has heard from positions 1 and 2 as if he was someone passing by and hearing them talk. How does he feel the situation could be resolved.

Now without breaking state, he returns to position 1 and says what he now feels about the limiting belief.

Here's another NLP technique for finding mislaid skills. It's called the Time Line. We used it in the last chapter on goal setting and it is great here as well.

1) Imagine a line on the floor stretching from the past into the future.
2) Ask him to stand on the point that for him represents today.
3) Ask him to think hard about what's going on in his life at the moment. What's going well and what would he like more of or what could be better still?
4) What skill does he think he needs now?
5) When and where did he have that skill? Go and stand on that place on the time line.
6) Now he needs to think hard about how he had that skill. See himself doing it, hear what is being said and feel what he felt. When the feeling is very strong, he needs to anchor it by making a circle with his thumb and first finger. When the feeling subsides, remove the anchor and break state. Repeat the process a few times until he feels he has a well established anchor for the skill.

7) Return to the point on the line representing the present and use the anchor to access that resource. Now does he feel more confident about the 11+?

8) Ask him to step into the future again and visualise himself having passed and anchor.

Resources that he can't find can be modelled and this is covered in the next chapter.

There are some toxic words to avoid; rephrase what you wanted to say without them.

1. **'can't'** – this is a limiting belief – what if he <u>could</u> do it, what would that also mean he could do?

2. **but** – anything you say before the word 'but' has no effect and everything after it is emphasised. If you say, 'I want you to do some 11+ homework but if you're too tired…' what you are really saying is he is too tired to do it.

3. 'always', 'never', 'everyone', 'no-one' and all other generalisations – these cannot be true so instead of saying something like 'everyone else will be practising their 11+ questions' reword it because that isn't true and he knows it so it will have little effect.

4. 'don't' – this word is very interesting. If I say to you 'don't think about pink elephants' what do you do? You think about pink elephants! This is because in order to make any sense of what I said, you need to imagine a pink elephant. Tell him what you <u>do</u> want not what you don't want.

CHAPTER 6: MODELLING EXCELLENCE

What is it?

There are a number of therapies that offer life coaching but what makes NLP different is this principle called 'modelling'.

Modelling is the copying of a skill you observe in someone else that you want for yourself along with the underlying belief that underpins it. Let me give you an example; let's say you want to help your child build skills he has observed in another child? Perhaps he envies a child who gets better marks or can read or spell well, knows his tables better or understands the non verbal reasoning questions? Here's what to do. Ask him to:

- Observe the skill.

- Be specific about what part of it he wants.

- Find several models of excellence of it.

- Notice the structure, how they do it step by step.

- Extract the underlying belief about the ability to do it. This means finding out what they believe about what they do. What thoughts do they have and what is their self talk.

- Practise it himself and take on the belief.

- Incorporate it into his repertoire of skills.

A skill can be as small as knowing his 9 times table, spelling long words, reading quickly, anything that he admires in someone else. Be curious with him about the skill and ask him to notice every aspect of it. How do they do it, what is the process?

Identify the exact nature of the skill. It's much easier to model something specific rather than something vague.

For example he might admire the way another child in his class gets top marks but that is too vague and there are many skills involved.

He needs to break down what he has observed into small parts and identify exactly what these are.

- Concentrating in class

- Knowing his tables

- Having a go

- Checking his answers

Help him to find examples of excellence for the precise skill. It could be that those who do that particular skill with excellence don't use it in the way he intends to use it but for the purposes of modelling this doesn't matter.

Spend time watching those with the skill and note down everything he observes. Practise whenever he can and be curious about the response he gets. Is it starting to work?

Some of his models will be easier to approach than others but with those who he feels confident with, he can ask them how they do the thing he is observing. He can be specific, 'You nearly always get your tables test right, how do you do that?'

It is not unusual for children not to know how they do something they do well because they do it quite naturally and it could be difficult to explain.

We need their underlying beliefs. Ask what the other child is thinking when he's doing what he does well.

If we use the analogy of the potter it may help explain why this is important. If you are watching a potter mould a lump of clay you can guess what he is making and you can copy what he does but you will only make the same thing as the potter if you know what the potter is imagining in his head about what form the clay will take.

Once he gets the self talk (belief) as well as the skill he can practise these for himself.

Beliefs are not values; they can be changed as we gather new information and experiences. For example, I don't suppose he believes in Father Christmas still does he?!

Ask him what skills he wants and from whom.

I want this skill   *From*

Now write down below what he could pass on to them.

Modelling is a great skill as it means he can be whatever he chooses to be if he believes he can do it and gets the skill either from where he has it within himself or from someone who models it with excellence.

CHAPTER 7: FEEDBACK AND REFRAMING TO STAY POSITIVE

One of the ways you can support your 11+ child is to encourage them to learn from feedback rather than feel downhearted.

The positive intention of feedback it to provide learning so that the next time they do that type of question they will get it right.

Use the 'feedback sandwich'.

What did they do well?

What could they have done <u>even</u> better?

What was good overall?

Viewing failure as feedback is reframing. It is looking at it in a different way, a positive way that we can learn from.

Here are some common pitfalls.

   1) Generalisations

These are when we tell them that they 'always' or 'never' do something, or when 'everyone else does/knows'.

This can't possibly be true and there is richer feedback in looking at the exceptions. For example, focus on the positive and notice when they did x and the result was excellent rather than the many times they did not and the result was unsatisfactory.

A classic example of a generalisation is 'I can't...' either verbalised or when you avoid the thing you think you 'can't do'. Many children avoid certain question types in the 11+ because they 'can't do them'. You can avoid this by helping them and letting them practise them until they can. It's not that they 'can't do them' they simply haven't learnt yet how to do them.

2) Deletions

In order for feedback to be helpful it needs to give detailed examples so they can learn from it. Simply telling them, 'You did much better on that practice paper' deletes the important detail about specifics from which they can learn.

How exactly did it go, what did they do differently and what will they do next time?

3) Distortions

There are three ways we can distort communication.

Assumptions –

When we assume we know their feelings e.g. 'you must be getting pretty nervous about the 11+ test next week' they may not be. Perhaps you are though and are projecting your angst onto them? Now you have put the idea into their head that they didn't have before.

Mind reading

Predicting the future can be unhelpful in a feedback scenario e.g. 'You'll be much happier once it's all over'. Well maybe they won't. You will be perhaps but maybe they will miss the attention?

Cause and effect

No-one can make you feel a particular way; that is your choice alone. Putting the responsibility for your feelings onto your child is a distortion e.g. 'You make me so angry when……….'.

CHAPTER 8: LITERACY

Type A (Chukra Type 10)

Your child needs to find the one letter that both ends the first word and starts the second word for both sets of two words.

They are multiple choice answers so the child has 5 options and he has to use the question sheet in conjunction with the answer sheet. So they will start with the first letter option and test each one until the find the one letter that works.

Example:

TRA ( ) ART   WAS ( ) OUND

Options given

Y

P

H

E

M

The answer is P which makes the words trap, part, wasp, pound.

Encourage your child to choose the letter that makes the most number of words because they may not be familiar with all four words so may not recognise them.

You can help your child best with Type A questions by encouraging them to build their vocabulary by reading and talking rather than watching TV.

Type B (Chukra Type 14)

Your child will be given 5 words and have to find the two words that are different from the other 3 and underline them. A common mistake is for the child to underline the three that are the same rather than the two that are different.

Example

rubbish   waste   waist   decline   refuse

Note that refuse can be pronounced two ways. With the emphasis at the beginning it means 'rubbish' and when the emphasis is at the end it means 'say no'. Just looking at the word, children may not realise that it has those two meanings. As it sits alongside the word 'decline' they could easily only think of 'refuse' meaning 'say no'. It is a synonym.

Note too that waist and waste sound the same but mean something different as well. They are homophones.

The correct answer is of course to underline waist and decline as the other three 'rubbish', 'waste' and 'refuse' have a similar meaning.

It is important in Type B questions for children to know the difference between nouns, verbs and adjectives because the three similar words will all be the same part of speech.

Noun – a thing eg pencil, socks, duvet

Verb – doing word eg to cry, to change, to take

Adjective – describing word eg artistic, wooden, sly

It is also important for them to understand how prefixes affect the meaning of the rest of the word.

'un' means opposite e.g. certain means to be sure and uncertain means not to be sure.

'ex' means going outwards so exit is going out, expand is getting bigger, exhale is breathing out. So any word beginning with 'ex' is going to be 'bigger than', 'more than', 'better than'.

'in' means something is coming inwards, getting smaller or less than, so 'interior' is inside, 'include' is to let someone join in, 'inferior' is less good

Type D (Chukra Type 13)

This question requires children to recognise words that have a similar meaning. They are presented with two sets of 3 words and have to select one from each set that means the same as one from the other set.

Example

(jump   leap   pond)   (pool   speak   talk)

How easy is it to see the two in the same set that mean the same eg 'jump' and 'leap' and 'speak' and 'talk'? Prepare children so they recognise the question type and know they need one from each set. Thus the correct answer is 'pond' and 'pool'.

They need to recognise nouns, adjectives and verbs as similar words must both be the same part of speech.

Parents can help by extending vocabulary. They can ask their children to put 2 different words into a sentence and look to see if it still conveys the same meaning.

Type E (Chukra Type 8)

Children are given a sentence within which is hidden a four letter word that will combine the end of one word of the sentence with the beginning of the next word.

Example : During the year my sister has grown three inches.

The best way to find the hidden word is to take your first finger of each hand and take two words at a time. Remember that it is a four letter word you are looking for so start by looking at the first and last 3 letters of each word. Then move your fingers so you look at each possible combination of four letters across the two words. It's probably easier to see on the photograph.

The 4 letter word will be found at the end of 1 word and the beginning of the next. You may find 1 letter, then 3 in the next word, 2 letters in each, or 3 letters then 1 in the next word.

Words beginning with vowels are especially difficult to find so writing a list of common 4 letter words beginning with vowels is worthwhile e,g, isle, echo, into.

Words such as 'tyre' are also difficult to find due to the 'y' in them. 'The' can only be followed by m, n, or y so these are common answers.

<u>Type F (Chukra Type 7)</u>

Children often find this question needs most practising.

They will be presented with a sentence where one word is in capitals.

<u>Example</u>

Mum was MING the broken toy.

In the answer sheet they will be given 5 possible 3 letter words that, inserted into the word in capitals, makes a real word that makes sense in the sentence.

Firstly the children must read the sentence and try to guess the word from the sense of the sentence.

Next they would see where the letters fitted in e.g. ing is a common word ending so it is likely it would be M...ING.

Lastly they would look at the answer sheet in conjunction with the question to see the 5 possible answers. Good spelling is needed and good visualisation of words. It is always worth writing down the word to see if the spelling is correct. You need to go through the list to see which one makes a word that makes sense. In this case it would be 'end' to make the word 'mending'.

Type H (Chukra Type 12)

This question presents two sets of words in brackets.

(up run walk)   (smile laugh down)

Your child needs to find one word from each set such that they are opposites. In this case 'up' and 'down'.

A child not correctly reading this question might spot words that are similar such as 'smile' and 'laugh' but the question asks for opposites.

They must also choose one word from each set of brackets.

This question requires children to know opposites and you can help him best again by encouraging reading and talking as well as learning unfamiliar words such as minority / majority, advance / retreat, prohibit / allow.

Opposites are never nouns and he should be aware of falling into the trap of choosing doctor/nurse, cat/dog, horse/cow as these are all incorrect but will appear on the answer sheet to tempt them into a wrong answer. Opposites are often adjectives e.g. happy/sad, rough/smooth, old/young.

Type J (Chukra Type 9)

This type of question involves moving a letter from the first word and placing it into the second word to make two new words.

Example

BLACK   TIE

Which letter can be taken from Black to make another word out of Tie yet leave a word?

The answer is to take the 'L out of BLACK to leave BACK and place the 'L' in tie to make TILE.

First he can place his pencil over each letter of BLACK and see which letters can be taken out. B, L can both be taken out to leave a complete word LACK, BACK.

Both letters can be written above the word. Then look at the second word and decide which of the 2 letters can be added to it to form a longer word

Taking a letter from one word to make another, requires children to visualise the letters in words and become familiar with what letters 'sit well' with another. For example with 'p', an 'l' sits well with it.

An 'l' is a brilliant letter to move from one word to another because you can have seven different letters that will sit in front of an 'l' so if you're struggling and there's an 'l' take it out , does it leave a word, 'yes' have I got something I can put it in front of ?

'w' is another good one because you can have 'sw' at the beginning of lots of words also 'ch', 'ph' , 'sh', or at the end a 'ck', they are letters that like to sit together. Two vowels often sit together in the middle of a word and can often be moved

Type M (Chukra Type 15)

This type requires him to spot a connection by finding two words, one from each group that will complete the sentence.

<u>Example</u>

Fish is to (chips scales cod)

As bird is to (feathers nest wing)

The connection is that a fish has scales and a bird has feathers (it is their body covering)

A complete list of connections can be learnt and applied:

Colours

Numbers

Collective nouns e.g. herd, flock, gaggle, pack,

Homophones,(words that sound the same) e.g. which, witch, quay, key

Palindromes (words that read the same forwards and backwards) e.g. madam, pip,

Similars and opposites

Anagrams,(words that can rearrange their letters to form another word e.g. pest and step

Different tenses

Animal's homes

Young animals

Masculine and feminine forms of words

Fruit

Vegetables.

It is a good idea when practising to write down the connection beside the question and see how many different ones you can find. There are only a certain number of different ones and they will begin to repeat themselves.

Type N (Chukra Type 3)

This question involves both literacy and codes.

Four words are written as you would expect, in standard English and underneath these you are presented with three words written in code.

The codes are not in the same order as the words and one of them is missing.

It is based on looking at the position of the numbers and finding the letter that relates to it.

<u>Example</u>

PAWS PEWS PEAR PEER

5164 5132 5632

Each number represents a letter.

As each word starts with 'P' and each coded set starts with '5' we know that 5=P.

Then choose a number that appears in at least 2 of the number codes, but preferably 3. He must look at the position of the number e.g. '1' is in second position so it must be 'e' as that is the only letter that appears twice in the second position.

Always write the words over the numbers as you only have to use 3 of the words, also it is more likely that you will write a word correctly but you may make a mistake writing down a number code.

Also, look out for 2 numbers that are the same in the middle of a sequence as this will tell you are looking for a word containing a double letter. If a number has the possibility of being more than one letter, move away from it and find a number that can only represent one letter.

Type O (Chukra Type 6)

In this question there are three pairs of words with the third pair incomplete. The challenge is to find the missing word.

Your child is required to move letters around in a certain sequence. No vocabulary or spelling is necessary.

Example: (dare read) (rage gear) (post ----)

Use only one side of the question (both sides will give you the same answer but avoid double letters if possible)

Look at READ – the 1st letter is R and comes from the 3rd letter in DARE, the 3rd letter in POST is S.

E is the 2nd letter in READ and is the last letter of DARE, the last letter of POST is T.

A is the 3rd letter of READ and the 2nd of DARE, the 2nd of POST is O.

The last letter of READ is D and it is the 1st letter of DARE, the 1st letter of POST is P, so the answer is STOP.

It is simply a matter of looking at the sequence of the letters in the first two words and applying 'the rule' to your answer.

Type Q (Chukra Type 11)

Again two sets of words in brackets are presented. Your child needs to take each word in turn from the set on the left and try them in front of the words on the right until he has found a compound word.

Example

(Motor gas electric) (engine bus cycle)

Take Motor from the first set and team it up with cycle to make the compound word 'motorcycle'.

A compound word is two separate words that we push together to make a longer word. We do this visually and put up our right hand and put up our left hand and we push our hands together like sliding doors so straight away they've got a visual, auditory and kinaesthetic understanding.

Examples are :

Butter fly	Butterfly
Green house	Greenhouse
Foot ball	Football

These are the simple ones.

Next we have those that when you push them together they don't sound the same

So up	Soup
Off ice	Office
Not ice	Notice
Beg in	Begin
Go at	Goat
So lid	Solid

111

Tips are to look for a 'th' in the middle of a word giving you a word ending in 't' and the second one beginning with 'h' , thus changing the sound of the two words.

Common compound word beginnings are: 'be' (belong, before, behind, become, begin) 'in' (insure, invest, income) 'con', 're','de' and 'dis'.

Common compound word endings are: 'ing', 'ice', 'tion', 'ly', 'sion' and 'ed',

Many of these are not complete words but will begin or end a longer word e.g. 'ing' will form the end of king, wing, sing, thing

Type R (Chukra Type 5)

This type is commonly confused with type O. You are given two sets of 3 words with a missing word in the second set.

<u>Example</u>

rusty   (rye)   stare

ghoul (?)   leafy

Look at the word 'rye' – it begins with 'r'.

'r' comes from the first letter of 'rusty' or the fourth letter of 'stare'.

Look on the 2nd line at letters in the same position – it will be either 'g' from ghoul or 'f' from 'leafy'.

Look at 'rye' again.

The second letter is 'y'.

That comes from last letter of 'rusty'. The last letter of 'ghoul' is 'l'.

Look at 'rye' again. The last letter is 'e' which comes from the end of 'stare'.

The end of 'leafy' is 'y' so the word we are looking for is either 'gly' or 'fly' so must be 'fly'.

This exercise is concerned with the position of letters in words and does not require any vocabulary.

Type S (Chukra Type 16)

This question offers us two pairs of words from which your child needs to find a word from the answer sheet that would fit with either set.

A wide vocabulary is necessary and a good understanding that words can be more than one part of speech. Coach (a bus) is a noun and coach (to teach) is a verb.

Example

(TEACH TRAIN) (BUS TRAM)

The answer book will offer 5 suggestions –

TELL INSTRUCT TROLLEY COACH RAIL

He must look at each word on the answer sheet to see which one can mean all the words in the brackets.

TEACH and TRAIN mean the same, as do BUS and TRAM, so if one of the words in the brackets is not known they can still attempt the question.

In this example the answer is 'COACH' which can mean a bus when it is a noun or 'to teach' when it is a verb.

Type Z (Chukra Type 21)

This question type is very lengthy and requires him to read the question carefully. The question is only worth one point so it is worth taking a guess at the answer and returning to it at the end of the paper if he has time.

Only read the information once and record as you go – it will take you too long to read it twice.

There are several different common types and all need to be worked out by writing down information.

If a question is written using words such as 'more than, less than' or 'above, below' he should record the information using a tower e.g. using initials for names, the person with the most would be at the top and so on

E (Emily had more than …..)

S (Susan had more than….but less than ….)

P (Peter had less than……)

Questions concerning times should be recorded by writing for example the times that people left and arrived (write over the names in the question rather than drawing a grid because it takes too long)

If a question is about the days of the week, write the initials of the days of the week M T W T F S S and use it as a number line to count along.

If you are given information regarding numbers; record the amount each person receives (e.g. how many sweets) by writing the number over the names written in the question. Add all the numbers together at the end and you will have the correct information to answer the question.

Read questions carefully – especially sentences such as Kate will be 7 <u>next year.</u>

CHAPTER 9: NUMERACY

Type G (Chukra Type 17)

Most children find is a nice easy place to start with your numeracy preparation.

Example

If A=3 B=4 C=6 D=7 E=14

What is the answer to the sum as a letter?

E – C + A – B =

Each letter has a value which should be written

above it so 14 will be written over E, 6 over C , etc.

The sum can then be worked out paying particular attention to the different mathematical signs.

Any working out can be done on the paper alongside the question but of course it is quicker if they are able to do it in their heads.

The answer will always be asked for as a letter so 7 becomes D.

Type I (Chukra Type 20)

You are presented with a sum with two sides. Both sides of the sum must add up to the same. Good mathematical skills are needed for this question but any working out can be written down by the question if necessary.

Example

18 − 5 + 7 = 40 + 3 - ?

Work out the first side which comes to 20 and write that over the sum. The second side must also equal 20 so add 40 and 3 to make 43, the next sign is a minus so he must insert 23 as this, taken away from the 43, will give the answer of 20 (the same as the first side.)

This is all about balancing and reading mathematical signs correctly. By writing 20 over both parts of the sum he will get a good visual picture of what he is trying to achieve.

Type P (Chukra Type 18)

This type is a number line which forms a pattern.

There are 4 different patterns to learn.

Example 1

1   2   4   7   11   16

Here the numbers are increasing. If you write down how much they increase each time you will see a pattern emerging. They increase by 1, 2, 3, 4, 5. So you now need to add on 6 to 16 to make the next number in the pattern 22. The number may also decrease but they will still form a pattern.

Example 2

20   17   18   18   16   19

As the numbers are increasing and decreasing in this line we need to look at alternate numbers. If we look at 20, 18, 16 we immediately see the pattern and we can see that the numbers decrease by 2 each time so the next number in the sequence will be 14.

Example 3

   7   8   14   16   21

Although there is a pattern to this sequence it is more complex. If he divides the numbers into pairs by putting brackets around them he will see that there is a gap of 1 between 7 and 8, a gap of 2 between 14 and 16 and there will then be a gap of 3 between 21 and the next number so the answer will be 24.

Example 4

   12   8   20   28   48

This again is a more complex pattern but one they need to understand and learn to recognise. If you add the first two numbers they will come to the sum of the third. Add the 2nd and 3rd number and it will come to the sum of the 4th. So to get the answer add the last 2 numbers (28 + 48) and you will get 76.

<u>TYPE K (Chukra Type 19)</u>

This is often considered the most challenging of the number questions.

<u>Example</u>

(10 { 14 } 5) (12 { 19 } 8) (15 {   } 10)

The 2 outside numbers are used to make the number in the centre. They can be added, subtracted, multiplied or divided. However, they may not come to the exact number so a 2nd mathematical application has to be added.

In the example 10 + 5 = 15 then a 1 is taken away to = 14. The same pattern is applied to the middle set 12 + 8 = 20 – 1 = 19.

The pattern is followed in the final part of the question 15 + 10 – 1 = 24

Once you have done the basic addition of the two outside numbers you may have to apply any of the following to get the middle number – halve , double add on a few, or take away a few. Another possibility is using one of the outside numbers twice e.g. (7 { 20 } 6) add 7 and 6, then add 7 in again to make 20.

CODE QUESTIONS

TYPE L (Chukra Type 1)

Codes always form patterns and require him to count along an alphabet line recognising the pattern. Letters are always written in upper case and he should write his answer in the same format as this is what will appear on the answer sheet. It is quicker to transfer an answer that is in the same format and does not have to be changed from lower to upper case. An alphabet line will always be provided.

He should use his left hand to follow the question and his right hand to count along the alphabet line. Counting towards Z is forward and towards A is backwards. Think of the alphabet as a never ending circle so when you reach Z continue counting to A.

<u>Example</u>

AV   BT   CR   DP

Split the letter groups down the middle with a faint line. Immediately you should see a pattern appear.

Look at A, B, C, D – this is counting forward one each time.

Look at V, T, R, P – if you count along with your pencil you will see that you are counting backwards in a pattern of two, so the answer is EN.

There are also mirror image codes where the alphabet is split down the middle so he needs to know the middle falls between M and N. The letter A will correspond to Z, C will correspond to X, etc.

<u>TYPE U (Chukra Type 4)</u>

This is a similar type and all the instructions above relate to this question in the same way.

FK is to CH

As   PR is to .....

Again split the letters. Count along the alphabet line with the pencil from F to C – this is three back. Move your pencil to P and count three back. This will bring you to M.

Count along again from K to H – this is three back. Move to R and count three back. This will bring you to O so the answer is MO.

TYPE C

This is a complex code question and takes the longest to complete. Again use your left hand to follow the question and your right hand with the pencil to count along the alphabet line.

Example

If the code for MISS is NLTV

What is the code for ACHE?

Underline the word ACHE. As ache is a word you need to identify the word on the line above (MISS). Put a dot over MISS and draw an arrow to NLTV. This tells you that you are working forwards, some questions require you to work backwards.

Count from M to N (1 forward), write down 1F, then from I to L (3 forward), write down 3F, then from S to T(1 forward) write down 1F. Don't count any more as you can see the pattern – 1F 3F 1F.

Look at ACHE. Count 1 forward from A (B), count 3 forward from C (F), count 1 forward from H (I), count 3 forward from E (H). Your answer is BFIH.

If you start from a word your answer will be a code and if you start from a code your answer will be a word.

CHAPTER 10: NON VERBAL REASONING

These question types require your child to study shapes and patterns, notice what is the same and what is different, what has been rotated, what is mirrored and what has reduced or increased in dimensions.

So I expect you've guessed it already, visualising is a core skill here. If you missed out that exercise in the first chapter, go back and do it now with your child because it will be enormously reassuring for him to realise he has the skills he needs already for non verbal reasoning.

How many fit inside?

Your child is given a shape and asked how many squares of a certain size would fit inside it. Like this.

How many squares like this ☐ are in the following shape?

The shape would not be presented like this with the squares already shown in it of course. The reason I have shown it like this is to show you how your child needs to visualise it. He needs to look at the shape 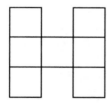 and imagine it replicated in the given figure.

Draw in all the squares or whatever shape you're given and then number them rather than risk counting them and missing one out.

Which shape is similar?

Your child will be given a series of three shapes which are similar in some way. They then have to choose from a further four shapes, which one fits with the first three.

He needs to look for patterns here. Questions to ask himself are: what type of shape are they, how many sides do they have, how many squares are in them, which are shaded/black/white?

First rule out the ones on the right that are obviously not a fit with the ones on the left and then start the process outlined above.

The answer above is D because the three on the left each have three sides.

<u>Find the shaded fraction</u>

The child has to find the shaded fraction by first checking that all the parts are of an equal size and shape. Sometimes this will mean that he has to draw lines inside the shape where an unshaded shape of a matching size would have been.

128

Count up all the parts first. In the figure below there are 12.

Then count up the shaded parts. There are 2. Then choose from the options given which is the correct fraction.

$\frac{1}{5}$ $\frac{3}{4}$ $\frac{2}{3}$ $\frac{1}{6}$

The answer is 1/6 because two out of the 12 parts are shaded.

<u>Which one is different</u>

Five shapes are presented of which one is different from the other four.

This applies the same principles as 'which shape is similar' so check for types of shapes, number of sides and position of shapes.

<u>Find the shaded fraction of equal value.</u>

This is similar to 'Find the shaded fraction' although for this one children need to know that 2/6ths is the same as 1/3rd and son on. So first add up all the shapes and then how many of them are shaded and write this as a fraction for each of the two figures shown.

Then find the correct equivalents.

<u>Where is it hidden</u>

Children have to find the shape shown within one of the four figures given. Check the number of sides in the hidden shape, the types of angles and the length of lines. Then look for it in one of the figures. You may have to rotate the shape to find it.

<u>What comes next</u>

In this one you are given a series of shapes, some shaded or changed, perhaps by size or rotation and decide which comes next in the sequence.

The next one in the pattern here would be a circle.

<u>Give the next number</u>

This is a numeracy pattern with a sequence of numbers increasing or decreasing, multiplied or divided.

Find the difference between each pair of numbers to find the pattern and predict what the next one will be.

45, 50, 55, 60, 65 (70)

The numbers are all increasing by 5, effectively your 5 times table.

Which shape is the same but facing the opposite direction

Here you are looking for the mirror image of the given figure. First cross out those that are obviously wrong then look at what you have left and check which of the options is an exact mirror image. Visualise a mirror to the right of the given image and visualise what its mirror image would look like.

How does it look folded in/ opened out

Visualisation is very important for this one. You can make shapes like the ones in practice papers and work them out by folding them up and unfolding them in order to prepare for this type of question.

Make sure you count the faces or flaps and check which ones are shaded or coloured.

What shape now after adding/subtracting

Here you are given two shapes which unchanged when added together or subtracted, make one of the possible figures given.

132

<u>Supply the missing numbers/ Fill in the addition table</u>

You will be given a sum where one of the numbers is missing and it can be a zero. This is straightforward maths and requires a sound knowledge of adding and subtracting.

<u>Which shape completes the matching pair</u>

Match the second pair of shapes in the same way as the first pair is matched.

  ?

In the above example you'd be choosing a black triangle.

<u>Which two shapes are exactly the same</u>

You are looking for identical shapes so ignore any that are obviously different and work on the rest. The shapes will have been rotated or mirrored so visualisation skills are really useful in this one.

EAT, SLEEP AND EXERCISE

It probably sounds obvious but the best way to prepare your child for the 11+ is to ensure he gets enough sleep, good food and plenty of exercise to stimulate those brain cells!

Children cannot work on an empty stomach so provide a nourishing snack before he starts work on any practice papers and aim for ten minute sessions daily, building up over the year until they are doing full practice papers a few months before the exam.

Look out for our 10 minutes a day 11+ app!

AND FINALLY

If there is anything you are unsure about or would like to work on, please get in touch with us judy@engagingnlp.com or via the website www.engagingnlp.com and I would be happy to explain further or arrange an NLP coaching session.

Lightning Source UK Ltd.
Milton Keynes UK
01 December 2010

163645UK00001B/79/P